12 INCREDIBLE FACTS ABOUT THE
BOSTON TEA PARTY

by Kristin Marciniak

12 STORY LIBRARY

www.12StoryLibrary.com

12-Story Library is an imprint of Peterson Publishing Company and Press Room Editions.

Produced for 12-Story Library by Red Line Editorial

Photographs ©: North Wind Picture Archives/AP Images, cover, 1, 16, 19, 24, 29; Library of Congress, 4, 6, 12, 13, 21, 22, 23, 27; North Wind Picture Archives, 8, 11, 15, 25; Bettmann/Corbis/AP Images, 9, 10, 17; bwzenith/iStock/Thinkstock, 14, 28; Brian Snyder/ Reuter/Corbis, 18; AP Images, 20

ISBN
978-1-63235-126-5 (hardcover)
978-1-63235-169-2 (paperback)
978-1-62143-221-0 (hosted ebook)

Library of Congress Control Number: 2015933981

Printed in the United States of America
Mankato, MN
June, 2015

Go beyond the book. Get free, up-to-date content on this topic at 12StoryLibrary.com.

TABLE OF CONTENTS

GREAT BRITAIN RULES AMERICAN COLONIES

It wasn't very long ago that Great Britain ruled most of North America. In 1765, the 13 American colonies all answered to the King of England, George III. The king was the head of the British government. He worked closely with Parliament. Parliament made the laws and rules for all of the British Empire.

King George III and Parliament didn't make all of the decisions in the colonies. Great Britain handled trade and other foreign affairs. The colonists took care of local matters, such as taxes and the local courts. They also had their own militias. These were small local armies.

Most Americans liked being part of the British Empire. Great Britain protected them from attacks by American Indians and foreign countries.

King George III ruled the 13 colonies.

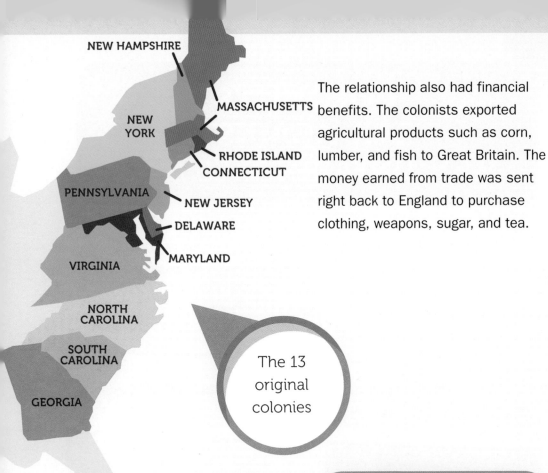

NEW HAMPSHIRE

MASSACHUSETTS

NEW YORK

RHODE ISLAND

CONNECTICUT

PENNSYLVANIA

NEW JERSEY

DELAWARE

MARYLAND

VIRGINIA

NORTH CAROLINA

SOUTH CAROLINA

GEORGIA

The 13 original colonies

The relationship also had financial benefits. The colonists exported agricultural products such as corn, lumber, and fish to Great Britain. The money earned from trade was sent right back to England to purchase clothing, weapons, sugar, and tea.

THE MISSING COLONY

There were 13 American colonies. But what about Maine? Maine was actually part of Massachusetts during this time. In the early 1800s, people living in Maine felt that they were ignored by the Massachusetts government. The two territories agreed to separate. Maine became its own state in 1820.

2.5 million

Approximate number of European settlers living in the 13 colonies in 1775.

- King George III was the leader of Great Britain.
- Parliament made the laws for the British Empire.
- Most Americans valued the protection and trade opportunities provided by Great Britain.

COLONISTS RAIL AGAINST UNFAIR TAXES

The British government spent millions to win the French and Indian War (1754–1763). A lot of that money was spent protecting the American colonies. Parliament wanted the colonists to pay some of the debt, so it imposed new taxes.

The Stamp Act of 1765 forced colonists to buy special stamped

This is the Place to affix the STAMP.

In protest of the Stamp Act, one publication printed a skull and crossbones instead.

THINK ABOUT IT

Compare the colonists' reactions to the Stamp Act and the Townshend Acts. Were the colonists successful in getting what they wanted? Why or why not?

£130 million

Britain's national debt after the French and Indian War.

- Parliament thought that colonists should pay some of their debt.
- The Stamp Act was passed in 1765 and lasted for only five months.
- The Townshend Acts were passed in 1767. All except the tea tax were repealed by 1770.

paper for official documents such as deeds and newspapers. The colonists didn't think this was fair. The colonists didn't have any representatives in Parliament. So they thought that they shouldn't have to pay taxes. They protested the Stamp Act by boycotting British goods. That hurt Great Britain's merchants. Parliament repealed the Stamp Act about five months later.

But Great Britain wasn't done taxing the colonists. The Townshend Acts were passed on November 20, 1767. They taxed English imports such as glass, tea, and paint. The members of the Massachusetts Legislature, the local government, were angered by another attempt at taxation without representation. They asked the other 12 colonies to protest the new taxes. In response, the British government shut down the Massachusetts Legislature.

The other colonial legislatures felt threatened by Great Britain's control over local government. All 12 joined the fight against the Townshend Acts. They were successful. By 1770, most of the taxes had been repealed. Only the tea tax remained.

TEA COMPANY ON VERGE OF COLLAPSE

The remaining tea tax was only three cents per pound of tea. That was less than one-tenth of one cent per cup. The tax was never meant to be a big moneymaker for the British. It was a symbol of control. It showed that the British government could tax anything in the colonies at any time. Many Americans responded by purchasing tea smuggled from the Dutch Republic. Some gave up tea altogether.

That was a problem for the East India Company. It was a British company that imported goods, including tea, from Asia and the Middle East. The company's owners had made some bad business

A fleet of ships owned by the East India Company

18 million

Weight, in pounds (8.5 million kg), of surplus tea the East India Company wanted to sell.

- Tea tax was a symbol of Great Britain's control over the colonies.
- Great Britain's East India Company was nearly bankrupt.
- Parliament passed the Tea Act of 1773 to boost colonial sales of British tea.

decisions. They had a lot of debts. If the company didn't increase its sales, it would go bankrupt.

Company officials thought colonists would buy tea if it was less expensive. They asked the British government to repeal the tea tax. Parliament said no. Instead it passed the Tea Act of 1773. That let the East India Company sell and ship tea directly to the colonies. The company was also freed from paying export taxes. Even with the tea tax, the overall price of tea in the colonies would go down. British tea would be less expensive than even the cheapest smuggled tea.

New York colonists react angrily to the announcement of the Tea Act.

9

COLONISTS INFURIATED BY LOW TEA PRICES

Colonial merchants were furious about the Tea Act. Those who sold smuggled Dutch tea were angry that British tea would be less expensive.

Others were mad that British tea could be sold only by merchants who had been selected by the king and were loyal to Parliament.

The merchants' anger spread to the public. The Tea Act of 1773 lowered the price of tea in the colonies, but it didn't get rid of the tea tax. The colonists were still being taxed without representation in Parliament.

The tea was on its way to several coastal cities, including Boston, Massachusetts. Colonists would be responsible for paying the customs fees even if they didn't drink tea. Accepting the delivery would mean that it was okay for Great Britain to tax the colonists. Angry colonists wanted to make sure that tea never reached the shore.

A letter from Pennsylvania opposing the tea tax

Colonial merchants depended on the money they made from selling their goods to colonists.

50

Percentage decrease in the cost of British tea after the Tea Act of 1773.

- Colonial merchants were angry that British tea was less expensive than Dutch tea.
- Colonists were upset that they were still being taxed by the British government.
- Allowing the tea to reach the shore would be a sign that Americans accepted Great Britain's taxes.

THE IMPORTANCE OF TEA

Tea was not very popular in the colonies. Less than one-third of colonists drank it every day. It was more popular in Great Britain, especially with the upper class. Colonial women, hoping to imitate British nobility, served tea during social calls. Tea symbolized the colonial desire to be seen as equals to Great Britain's finest.

SECRET SOCIETY LEADS REBELLION

The Sons of Liberty was a group of men who opposed Great Britain's involvement in the colonies. They organized protests of British laws, starting with the Stamp Act in 1765.

Eventually there were chapters of the group in every colony. The names of most members remain a secret. But some leaders are well known even today.

Samuel Adams is believed to have founded the Boston chapter of the Sons of Liberty. He began his political career as a tax collector. This made him an expert on Great Britain's tax laws. Adams was the first colonial leader to argue against taxation without representation. His writings and speeches fueled Americans' anger towards the British government.

John Hancock was another Sons of Liberty member. Unlike other wealthy Americans, Hancock believed the colonies should be independent from Great Britain. He helped colonists avoid Great Britain's

Samuel Adams was against taxation without representation.

import taxes by smuggling goods into America on his boats. While Adams supported violent protest, Hancock thought the most lasting changes were made through politics. He is known for being the first person to sign the Declaration of Independence.

THINK ABOUT IT

Compare the descriptions of Samuel Adams and John Hancock. How are the two men similar? How are they different?

John Hancock believed the colonies should separate from Great Britain.

1765

Year that the Sons of Liberty was founded.

- The Sons of Liberty was a secret organization that protested British policies in the colonies.
- The Boston chapter of the group was led by Samuel Adams.
- Both Samuel Adams and John Hancock were early supporters of independence from Great Britain.

SONS OF LIBERTY BULLY TEA AGENTS

The Boston Sons of Liberty tried everything to stop the British tea from reaching shore. They demanded that the king's tea agents in the colonies resign their positions. The agents refused. Then the Sons insisted that any tea be shipped back to London. Again, the agents refused.

The first of four boats carrying tea arrived on November 28, 1773. Nearly 5,000 Bostonians gathered at the Old South Meeting House to protest its arrival. The meeting continued the next day. It was agreed that the tea should not leave the ships.

That was a problem for the ships' owners and captains, all of whom were American. It was illegal for a ship to leave harbor without unloading its cargo. The tea had to be unloaded and duties paid within 20 days.

The Old South Meeting House still stands in Boston.

BOSTON, December 2, 1773.

WHEREAS it has been reported that a Permit will be given by the Custom-House for Landing the Tea now on Board a Veſſel laying in this Harbour, commanded by Capt. HALL : THIS is to Remind the Publick, That it was ſolemnly voted by the Body of the People of this and the neighbouring Towns aſſembled at the Old-South Meeting-Houſe on Tueſday the 30th Day of *November*, that the ſaid Tea never ſhould be landed in this Province, or pay one Farthing of Duty : And as the aiding or aſſiſting in procuring or granting any ſuch Permit for landing the ſaid Tea or any other Tea ſo circumſtanced, or in offering any Permit when obtained to the-Maſter or [...] the ſaid Ship, or any other Ship in the ſame Situation, m[...] inhuman Thirſt for Blood, and will alſo in a great Meaſure acc[...] fuſion and Civil War : This is to aſſure ſuch public Enemies of [...]

A flyer warning colonists against buying tea

If not, the British government could seize the ships and their cargo.

By mid-December, three of the four ships were floating in Boston Harbor.

342

Number of chests of tea on the three ships in Boston Harbor.

- The Sons of Liberty tried to get the tea agents to resign.
- Bostonians voted to prevent the tea from being unloaded from the ships.
- It was illegal for the ships to leave the harbor without unloading the tea and paying duties.

The tea couldn't return to England, but it wasn't going to enter Boston, either. The Sons of Liberty decided the time for talking was done. Now it was time for action.

THINK ABOUT IT

Imagine that you are living in Boston in 1773. How would you explain to a friend the problems faced by the colonists, the British, and the captains of the ships carrying the tea?

SONS OF LIBERTY DISGUISE THEMSELVES

Another 5,000 Bostonians gathered in Old South Meeting House on Thursday, December 16, 1773. They tried to convince one of the ships' owners to send his boat back to England. He said he couldn't. British soldiers at Castle William wouldn't let the ship pass without paying the duties owed on the cargo. Massachusetts Governor Thomas Hutchinson agreed with the British soldiers.

The crowded room was in an uproar. Samuel Adams ended the meeting by saying, "This meeting can do no more to save the country." He was answered by a loud war-whoop. People poured out of the Meeting House to find 50 men dressed as Mohawk Indians outside.

These men were actually members of the Sons of Liberty. They'd painted their faces with soot. They wrapped themselves in wool blankets. Each man carried an axe or a gun. They headed to

Thomas Hutchinson

Tea Party participants disguised themselves as Mohawk Indians.

16

Number of teenagers known to have participated in the Boston Tea Party.

- More than 5,000 Bostonians were furious after the governor refused to let the ships leave the harbor.
- After the meeting, 50 members of the Sons of Liberty disguised themselves as Americans Indians.
- They headed to the docks to dump the tea in the harbor.

the docks. They planned to throw all of the British tea into Boston Harbor.

The men weren't trying to fool anybody. They knew they didn't look like actual American Indians. The costumes were meant to disguise their identities. They couldn't be charged with a crime if nobody knew who they were. The men also felt that dressing up like the native people showed that they thought of themselves as native people too.

SONS OF LIBERTY CALMLY DUMP TEA INTO HARBOR

On December 16, 1773, the dark streets of Boston were silent as the disguised men marched toward the harbor. One thousand onlookers followed behind. People were eager to see what would happen once the 50 men reached the boats.

Thirty members of the governor's Corps of Cadets stood guarding the harbor. They let the Sons of Liberty board the three ships. The cadets were the governor's army. But their commander was John Hancock. They, too, were in on the plan. All 80 men quickly got to work.

The Sons of Liberty politely requested the keys from the ships' captains. They carefully removed the tea chests from the cargo hold. Then they split open the chests with tomahawks and axes. All 342 chests were heaved into the harbor. Trails of tea leaves floated to the water's surface.

The mission was over in three hours. Nearly £10,000 worth of tea had been destroyed. That's approximately $1 million in today's money. All the other cargo was left

A tea chest from the Boston Tea Party

Tea chests were hacked open with tomahawks and axes.

untouched. There were no outbursts of violence. The Sons of Liberty disappeared into the night just as quietly as they had arrived.

92,000

Approximate amount, in pounds (41,730 kg), of the tea dumped into Boston Harbor on December 16, 1773.

- The costumed Sons of Liberty were joined by the Corps of Cadets aboard the three ships.
- The men were calm and quiet as they hacked open the tea chests and dumped them into the water.
- In all, 342 chests of tea were destroyed.

THE TEA CHESTS

The tea chests were from China. Each chest was built by hand and painted with special designs. Only two of the 342 chests still exist today. One is at the Daughters of the American Revolution Museum in Washington, DC. The other is at the Boston Tea Party Ships and Museum in Boston.

BRITISH SOLDIERS WATCH IN SILENCE

The Sons of Liberty had good reason for being quiet as they dumped the tea into Boston Harbor. They were afraid of being caught. There were British soldiers at nearby Castle William. They had been stationed in Boston since 1768, acting as a police force after the protests against the Townshend Acts. The British naval fleet was even closer. Their ships were just one-fourth of a mile (0.4 km) away from the tea-carrying cargo ships.

Even though the colonists were quiet, the British soldiers and sailors knew what was going on across the harbor. The commander at Castle William prepared his men to interrupt the tea party. But the order to go to shore never came. The Royal Navy, too, could only watch as chest after chest was thrown into the water. A navy admiral rowed a small boat to shore to get a better look at the action. He exchanged a few insults with some of the disguised men, but that was it.

The British had good reason for not stepping in. It was simply too

British soldiers occupied Castle William.

dangerous. The three cargo ships were docked at the wharf, close to the enormous crowd of onlookers. Firing at the Sons of Liberty would have risked the lives of innocent people. That would have made the colonists even angrier. The British weren't looking to start a war over tea.

10,000
Approximate number of people living in Boston in the mid-1700s.

- The Sons of Liberty worked quickly and quietly so as not to be caught by the British.
- The British army and navy watched as the tea was tossed into the water.
- The British didn't stop the tea party because there was a risk of harming onlookers.

Thousands of people watched the Boston Tea Party.

TEA PARTY FAILS TO UNITE ALL THE COLONIES

Boston wasn't the only city fighting the Tea Act. Several other New England cities also banned British tea. Some cities told colonists to stop drinking tea altogether. Ports in New Hampshire refused to accept ships carrying British tea. New York patriots succeeded in getting their local tea agents to resign.

Paul Revere brought the news of the Boston Tea Party to Philadelphia. Word spread to the rest of the colonies. Soon ships carrying British tea were greeted by angry colonists. By the end of April 1774, tea had been dumped and burned all across New England.

Not everyone supported the tea party. Property owners, especially those in the South, did not agree with the destruction of private property. Virginian George Washington said the Sons of Liberty were vandals. He, and most of Virginia, had been drinking tea since the repeal of the Townshend Acts in 1770. They would continue to do so through 1774.

Paul Revere spread the news of the tea party to Philadelphia.

80,000

Weight, in pounds (36,287 kg), of tea consumed by Virginians in 1773.

- News of the Boston Tea Party quickly spread throughout the colonies.
- Other New England cities joined the rebellion and held their own tea parties.
- Land owners, including many Southerners, didn't support the destruction of private property.

DESTROYED BY INDIANS.

YE GLORIOUS SONS OF FREEDOM, brave and bold,
That has ftood forth----fair LIBERTY to hold ;
Though you were INDIANS, come from diftant fhores,
Like MEN you acted----not like favage Moors.
CHORUS.
Boftonian's SONS keep up your Courage good,
Or Dye, like Martyrs, in fair Free-born Blood.
Our LIBERTY, and LIFE is now invaded,
And FREEDOM's brighteft Charms are darkly fhaded :
But, we will STAND---and think it noble mirth,
To DART the man that dare opprefs the Earth.
Boftonian's SONS keep up your Courage good,
Or Dye, like Martyrs, in fair Free-born Blood.
How grand the Scene !----(No Tyrant fhall oppofe)
The TEA is funk in fpite of all our foes.
A NOBLE SIGHT---to fee th' accurfed TEA
Mingled with MUD----and ever for to be ;
For KING and PRINCE fhall know that we are FREE.
Boftonian's SONS keep up your Courage good,
Or Dye, like Martyrs, in fair Free-born Blood.
Muft we be ftill--- and live on Blood-bought Ground,
And not oppofe the Tyrants curfed found ?
We Scorn the thought- ---our views are well refin'd
We Scorn thofe flavifh fhackles of the Mind,
" We've Souls that were not made to be confin'd."
Boftonian's SONS keep up your Courage good,
Or Dye, like Martyrs, in fair Freeborn Blood.
Could our ---fathers rife from their cold Graves,
And --- ir Land, with all their Children SLAVES ,
hey fay ! how would their Spirits rend,
er-ftrucken, to their Graves defcend.
ian's SONS keep up your Courage good,
ye, like Martyrs, in fair Free-born Blood.
h hearts of fteel now ftand the taſk.
all darkfome ways, nor wear a Mask.
ur noble Zeal fupport our frame,
ll Tyrants with eternal SHAME.
SONS keep up your Courage good,
nk all Tyrants in their GUILTY BLOOD.

A poem written in honor of the Boston Tea Party

SPREADING THE WORD

Word about the Boston Tea Party spread to other colonies through newspapers. There were 38 newspapers in America in the early 1770s. Most of them were published weekly. They printed local news, as well as articles and letters about what was happening in other colonies. They even published international news. Newspapers were the fastest, and sometimes only, way people could find out what was happening outside their hometowns.

23

11

GREAT BRITAIN FIGHTS BACK WITH PUNISHING LAWS

The Boston Tea Party was a great insult to the British government. King George was outraged. He said the colonies needed to be shown just how much they relied on Great Britain. Parliament had long discussions about going to war. Some members wanted to completely destroy Boston.

But many British people thought a war with America would be too expensive. Still, they felt a harsh punishment was necessary. Figuring out who to punish was more difficult. The Sons of Liberty took great care to hide their identities. They promised to never share the names of their fellow patriots. So the British government decided to punish all Bostonians with a series of new laws called the Coercive Acts.

More British soldiers arrived in Boston to enforce the Coercive Acts.

FRANCIS AKELEY

Despite best efforts, one of the Sons of Liberty was caught. Francis Akeley, a wooden wheel repairman, was put in jail for his involvement in the Boston Tea Party. He was 42 years old. He was eventually released and died two years later at the Battle of Bunker Hill.

4

Number of laws in the Coercive Acts that were passed to punish all Bostonians after the Boston Tea Party.

- Parliament considered going to war, but instead passed laws to punish all of Boston.
- Local government lost most of its power.
- Boston's port was closed to all trade.

Under the Coercive Acts, citizens of Massachusetts no longer had the right to trial by local jury. If someone committed a serious crime, they could be tried in another colony or even in England. Citizens could no longer vote for government representatives. Local government lost most of its power. British soldiers sent to Boston were allowed to stay in taverns and empty houses. Worst of all, Boston's ports were closed until the East India Company was paid back for the ruined tea.

British troops occupied Boston and other colonial cities.

TEA PARTY KICK-STARTS AMERICAN REVOLUTION

The Coercive Acts were a huge blow to the citizens of Boston. The closing of Boston's ports severely hurt the city's economy. Goods were shipped to Salem, Massachusetts, then transported 16 miles (26 km) on land to get to Boston. That was expensive. Many people, especially those who lost their jobs at the wharf, couldn't afford it.

Many in Boston felt that the punishment for the Boston Tea Party was greater than the actual crime. Fewer than 100 people had taken part in the tea party, but the entire city was being punished. Bostonians felt humiliated by King George and Parliament. Many realized for the first time that the British government did not see them as equals.

The people of Massachusetts supported Boston. Even many of those who disagreed with the tea party felt Parliament was wrong. Colonists in surrounding towns forced royal officials to flee their homes. Illegal town meetings were held. Juries refused to serve. British soldiers and Americans clashed throughout the colony.

10
Number of years between the Boston Tea Party and the end of the American Revolution.

- Many colonists felt that the punishment for the tea party was greater than the crime itself.
- The Coercive Acts severely hurt Boston's economy.
- Colonies united in their support of Boston.

Anger spread through New England and into the South. During the summer of 1774, every colony except Georgia elected leaders to a Continental Congress in Philadelphia. At this meeting, colonists planned to discuss how to fight back against Parliament's policies. It was the first time that individual colonies united against British rule. It was far from the last. The Boston Tea Party had sparked the American Revolution.

THINK ABOUT IT

How did the Boston Tea Party lead to the American Revolution? Use information from this book to answer this question.

Colonists faced off against the British in the first battle of the war—the Battle of Lexington.

12 KEY DATES

November 1, 1765
Stamp Act takes effect in the colonies.

March 18, 1766
Stamp Act is repealed.

November 20, 1767
Townshend Acts take effect in the colonies.

April 12, 1770
All of the Townshend Acts are repealed except for the tea tax.

May 10, 1773
Parliament passes the Tea Act.

November 2, 1773
The Boston Sons of Liberty demand that the tea agents resign.

November 18, 1773
Sons of Liberty again ask tea agents to resign.

November 28, 1773
The first tea ship arrives in Boston Harbor. Five thousand people meet at the Old South Meeting House and vote to keep the tea on the ship.

December 16, 1773
Sons of Liberty dump 342 chests of tea into Boston Harbor.

April 1774
All across New England colonists dump and burn British tea.

June 1, 1774
The Boston ports are closed under the Coercive Acts.

September 5, 1774
The First Continental Congress meets in Philadelphia, Pennsylvania.

GLOSSARY

bankrupt
Unable to pay debts.

boycotting
Refusing to buy, use, or participate as a means of protest.

chapter
People from a certain area who make up one part of an organization.

deeds
Legal documents related to property ownership.

disguise
To change the appearance of someone or something.

empire
A group of states or countries under one ruler.

export
A product that is made in one country and is sold in another.

patriots
People who strongly support their country.

repeal
To end or take back a law.

resign
To give up a job or position.

revolution
An attempt by many people to end the rule of a government.

seize
To take something.

smuggle
To illegally and secretly move something from one country to another.

wharf
A structure built on the shore so ships can unload cargo and passengers.

FOR MORE INFORMATION

Books

Brennan, Linda Crotta. *The Boston Tea Party: A History Perspectives Book.* North Mankato, MN: Cherry Lake Publishing, 2013.

Jeffrey, Gary. *Samuel Adams and the Boston Tea Party.* New York: Gareth Stevens Publishing, 2011.

Landau, Elaine. *The Boston Tea Party: Would YOU Join the Revolution?* New York: Enslow Elementary, 2014.

Morley, Jacqueline. *You Wouldn't Want to Be an American Colonist! A Settlement You'd Rather Not Start.* Danbury, CT: Children's Press, 2013.

Websites

Boston Tea Party Ships & Museum: Boston Tea Party Facts
www.bostonteapartyship.com/boston-tea-party-facts

Liberty's Kids: The Boston Tea Party
www.libertyskids.com/story/101.html

Old South Meeting House
www.oldsouthmeetinghouse.org

INDEX

About the Author

Kristin Marciniak writes the books she wishes she'd read in school. She most enjoys researching and writing about topics she previously knew nothing about. She studied journalism at the University of Missouri and lives in Kansas City.